SCHIRMER'S LIBRARY OF MUSICAL CLASSICS

Vol. 1512

JOHANN SEBASTIAN BACH

Fifteen Two-Part Inventions

For the Piano

Edited by

FERRUCCIO BUSONI

English Translation by

FREDERICK H. MARTENS

A Second-Piano Part to the
Fifteen Two-Part Inventions
by Louis Victor Saar is published by G. Schirmer, Inc.

G. SCHIRMER, Inc.

DISTRIBUTED BY

HAL•LEONARD®
CORPORATION

7777 W. BLUEMOUND RD. P.O. BOX 13819 MILWAUKEE, WI 53213

PREFACE TO THE FIRST EDITION

A closer examination of the usual system generally followed in teaching music has convinced me that Bach's *Inventions*, in most cases, are made to serve the needs of the piano beginner only as dry, technical material; and that the piano teacher seldom exerts himself to awaken in his pupils an understanding of the profounder meaning of these Bach creations.

Ordinarily study of the *Inventions* is confined to a *selection* from among them, made without system, and the frequent use of incorrect or poorly revised editions, their signs of ornamentation and expression-marks quite unreliable, is only calculated to increase the student's difficulty in realizing Bach's spirit and meaning. Finally, there is the important *compositional* aspect, which is entirely ignored in teaching, whereas it is calculated—more than any other—to develop the student's purely *musical* side and strengthen his critical acumen.

When so advanced a thinker as Bach here expresses his intention of revealing *a clearly marked style*, in order, *at the same time, to realize a strong foretaste of the composition*, we may take for granted that the Master followed a well thought-out plan in writing his work; and that each individual combination occurring therein has its own secret meaning and importance.

It is in order to make this meaning and importance more generally comprehensible that I have undertaken the task of preparing my version.

FERRUCCIO BUSONI.

Moscow, 1891.

The principal points taken into account in this edition are those which follow:

(1) An unequivocal presentation of the text throughout the work. (In particular with regard to clarity, the execution of ornaments and the distribution of the middle parts in the three-part movement.)

(2) The choice of an adequate fingering. (Especially with regard to the employ of the thumb and of the little finger on the black keys and finger sequence for diatonic figures with thumb held down):

    (a) Ascending with 3 4 3—4 5 4—4 5 3 4—4 5 2 3, etc.
    (b) Desending with 5 4 5—4 3 4—4 3 5 4—3 2 5 4, etc. Use of the "parallel" finger 1 3—2 4—3 5 3 1—4 2—5 3 in diatonic progressions and trills. Avoidance of change of finger on a sustained tone.

(3) Indications of tempo. N. B.—The Italian and English indications of tempo are intended to *supplement* rather than translate each other, in so far as the Italian mode of expression often is stiff and conventional, i. e., not sufficiently capable of conveying shadings; while English, on the other hand, cannot always supply certain definitely accepted conceptions as, for instance, *allegro, andante*.

(4) The expression-marks, meant to serve as a guide to the correct conception of Bach's style, which is characterized, above all, by virility, energy, breadth and grandeur. The soft shadings, the use of the pedal, the *arpeggiando*, the *tempo rubato*, even too smooth a *legato* and too frequent a *piano*—since they are not in keeping with the character of Bach's music—should be avoided, generally speaking.

(5) A commentary which—in addition to the hints on piano technic and remarks concerning interpretation—is intended, first of all, to supply a contribution to the *study of form*.

PREFACE TO THE SECOND EDITION

When to-day I consider this work which took shape some twenty years ago, it impresses me as one definitely completed, and I have decided, despite various changes of opinion on my part, to have it reissued *without alterations*.

I must warn the student against seeking to carry out my "interpretations" too literally. It is here that the moment and the individual may lay claim to rights of their own. My conception may be used as a reliable guide which those to whom some other valid path is known need not employ.

In the case of most of the Inventions there is, probably, but one road to follow; with regard to the interpretation of certain ones I myself do not now feel as I formerly did.

Thus it seemed to me in better taste to play the theme of the eighth three-part invention with a *single legato slur;* the eleventh, however, I would now shape more suavely, and would phrase the last as follows:

At present I change fingers on repeated notes little or not at all (and this applies as well to inverted mordents and mordents) and increasingly avoid the passing under of the thumb.

Finally, I no longer devote too much attention to unimportant details and incidental features, and consider the expression of a face more important than the cut of its features.

FERRUCCIO BUSONI.

Berlin, July, 1914.

33221

To the Music Institute in Helsingfors,
The Editor

Fifteen Two-Part Inventions

Edited by F. B. Busoni

English version by
Frederick H. Martens

Johann Sebastian Bach

Allegro
With animation and decision

(1) That a ♯ preceded the C on the second eighth-note of the measure is almost invariably forgotten by the pupil. Experience has dictated the advisability of repeating the ♯ before the second C♯ to be played.

(1a) In order to avoid the collision of both thumbs on the same key, the place of the bracketed E in the left hand may be taken by a sixteenth-rest.

(2) The same as at (1).

(3) The establishment of the principal key is sufficiently pronounced in the second measure before the last to make superfluous any holding back in the tempo of the measure before the last, where the imminence of the following close is clearly expressed.

(4) The inexplicable *arpeggiando*-sign, which accompanies this final chord in numerous editions, is in absolute contradiction to the virile style of the composition, and so far as regards Bach, must be termed a stylistic error. We wish to warn students, in particular, against effeminization of this kind, here and in analogous places.

N. B. With regard to the *form* of this piece, it is in the main so arranged that it may be called a *three-part* invention. The half-measure theme: (the bracketed eighth-note is treated freely, as an interval) underlies the entire composition; the closing formulas alone, which invariably terminate one of the three sections (indicated by double-bars *), testify to the non-employ of the principal theme. The theme first appears four times in alternation in the upper and lower parts, and then, in a quadruple sequence of its *inversion,* carries out a downward progression in the upper part; which progression at the same time accomplishes the modulation to the dominant key. In the fifth measure the sequential extension of the second half of the theme finally leads to the dominant cadence on which the first section ends. The second section (cadencing in the relative key) is almost entirely symmetrical in relation to the first, in which both parts exchange rôles. The intercalated third and fourth measures — a free, symmetrical imitation of the two preceding ones — have chiefly a modulatory significance. This duplication of the two initial measures in section two assumes organic shape in the *third* section, where the theme, alternating by measures, appears in its original form as well as in contrary motion. Worthy of notice, in this instance, is this transformation of the eighth-note movement, hitherto used, of the "counter-phrase" (the counterpoint led over the theme) into a tied half-note; and the subsequent inversion of the originally descending, but now (by a triple interlocking of the type theme) *ascending* movement, which triumphantly leads back into the principal key.

Incisive, rhythmic playing will most adequately express this model worklet.

---

* Double-bars have been used in each of the 30 Inventions to indicate the close of the individual sections.

Moderato

Expressively, but not dragging

2

dolce, semplice

(1) N.C. = new counterpoint, must be regarded in this instance only as a harmonic necessity, to make the transition to the dominant more evident. In accordance with the general basic conception of the form here presented the **A** in the lower voice might otherwise appear *uncovered* while the upper voice rests.

(2) Actually and originally the second eighth once appears as follows:

(3) For technical reasons which are self-evident the inverted mordent on D has been omitted.

(4) F.C. = free close.

N.B. The entirely novel imprint given this invention — compared with its predecessor — in form, character and content, makes a corresponding difference in presentation essential. Before all else, in this invention, it is the *canonical* aspect, usually overlooked, which must be clearly and comprehensively revealed, and on the correct presentation of which recognition of its form depends.

The two-measure phrase (**A**) which takes the place of the theme at the beginning is repeated in the third and fourth measures of the second part in the lower octave, whereas the part progresses contrapuntally (**B**) above it. This counterpoint (**B**), in turn, is treated in the same manner in the lower part, and a *new* counterpoint (**C**) is built up upon it. Thus, in succession — two measures at a time — **D** is placed above **C**, **E** above **D**. The upper part, in consequence, takes shape as an uninterrupted, continuous ten-measure movement, developed by the linking of **A**, **B**, **C**, **D** and **E**; and, two measures later, this starts in the lower part. Since both parts, however, conclude their imitative course with the tenth measure at the same time, the phrase **E** has to be dropped in the imitating part. On the other hand, the lower part sets in *first* in the second section, and the entire sequence is repeated in the subdominant key and in an inversion of the double counterpoint for another ten measures.

* The two measures which now follow serve to effect the modulatory return to the tonic, and, so to say, stand on neutral ground, *between* Section II and the abruptly closing Section III.

Vivace, quasi allegro
Vivaciously and forcefully

3

(1) Although this measure unquestionably must be regarded as forming part of the *theme*, the figure: nevertheless, is of slight significance because — save in the analogous case in Section III—it only appears *once* more in the course of the composition and then at 1ᵃ.

(2) At a more rapid tempo — the interpretation admits of various shadings in the movement of tonal groups— the editor would advise that the passage be simplified, as follows: The rhythmic and melodic outlines never should sound blurred.

(3) The thematic progression by seconds takes a leap of a third at +.

(4) In the working-out, three sixteenth-notes are placed before the two up-beat sixteenth-notes of the theme, whereby the following figure results: This version is also used in the Coda.

N. B. With the same strictness observed in exactly holding down the key in the case of sustained tones, the importance of the *rest,* on the other hand, also should be taken into account, by a corresponding raising of the hands. The unoccupied hand (i. e., the *left*) is inclined to remain on the key, a habit which frequently results in the creation of unintentional organ-points, and hence should be suppressed at the very start. This observation applies to similar places in all the Inventions and is of importance with regard to their *interpretation.*

---

* +−+ Actually: transitional measures from the second to the third sections (see note, * to preceding invention).

8

(1) The "staccato" here called for should approximate on the piano the effect produced on the violin by the use of the "thrust" bowing. The prescribed time-value of the note should be mulcted only to the extent required to carry out a short, energetic movement of the wrist, before striking the following key.

(2) In order correctly to visualize the thematic structure, it is advisable to think of this figure as paralleling the beginning of Section II; somewhat as follows:

(3) The above trill with minor second, in Bach's sense, is entirely correct and in style, even though the "crossrelationship" to the upper part arising from it may give offence to hyperpuritanical musical ears. The trill in reality takes the place of the descending melodic minor scale; the theme concatenation moving above it the same scale ascending.

(4) The measure here intercalated, symmetrically akin to the close of the first section, already forecasts the end of the piece, so that one is inclined to consider the four measures which still succeed it as a Coda.

Allegro risoluto
Rapidly, forcefully and passionately

(1) The principal figure of the theme must be "hammered out," so to say, in the sturdiest *non legato*. The manner of execution here indicated will give an approximate portrayal of the character of this interpretation.

(2) The sixteenth-note figures of the counter theme, on the other hand, should flow along in the most equalized *legato*. The three figures which relieve each other have a tendency to confuse, at first, because of their similarity. Hence the player will do well to reduce them to rule by a comparison of their recurrence: This will notably aid his memory while, on the other hand, technical practice of the figure sequence will powerfully further finger control.

(3) The theme itself comprises four full measures, then undergoes an imitation in the dominant, and is finally used in fragmentary form for an ascending three-measure sequence. The second section corresponds in all ways to the first, with the sole exception that in it the sequence *descends* instead of **ascending.**

(4) The Editor regards the four measures which follow as the first half of the theme and its imitation in the tonic. Another, less justified conception would be: to connect the preceding last measure of Section II with the fourth measure of Section III (in a single sequence) and to regard all that lies between as an "extension":

(5) A broader *ritenuto* which, incidentally, seems quite in place, calls for an enrichment of the trill:

N. B. This number is the first of those two-part Inventions in which the countersubject plays an *obligato* rôle, those in which one and the same *counter theme* (counterpoint to the theme) is retained throughout the composition, and appears as the theme's inseparable companion. Numbers 6, 9, 11 and 12 also are inventions of this type. We have here called attention to this peculiarity once and for all.

Allegretto piacevole, quasi Andantino
With graceful movement, not rapidly

6

(1) This figure, in the Editor's opinion, should sound out in strict rhythm, not too *legato* and innocent of that modern elegance which, somehow, is not compatible with Bach's style. The alternative phrasing (in which, as a rule, the two thirty-second-notes are slightly hurried in tempo) therefore should be rejected.

(2) The *legato* in the upper part can be secured only by using the pedal as indicated.

(3) What has been said at (1) applies here in the fullest sense.

(4) The phrasing indicated is intended to suggest the *thematic* relation between this and the following parallel measures.

N. B. This invention, above all others, is the only one in which the end of the first section, in the original edition, is indicated by a double-bar. We have refrained from similarly marking Sections II and III at this point (indicated by the N. B.), in order not to cause confusion, in view of the fact that the repetition-mark at the close applies to *both sections together.*

The two-part song— it might be called an intermezzo for flute and violoncello in a pastoral cantata— captivates by reason of its gentle melodic charm, and the spontaneity of its contrapuntal movement; if various kinds of touch are employed in playing, it becomes a useful study for performance. It might be remarked, incidentally, that the third section is a contrapuntal inversion of the first, i. e., that save for a few variants which result from the continuation in the principal key, it represents a change of rôle on the part of the two voices.

Allegro moderato ma deciso
Quite lively and with decision

7*

* In view of its form and nature, this invention might be classed as a kind of *primary invention* which had attained a "higher stage of development."

Ossia

N. B. In contrapuntal movements the entrance of the organ-point on the dominant may always be accepted as a signal for the beginning of the *last section*. It is all the more so in this particular instance, since from this moment on the principal key is not again abandoned. The figure: and what follows should be regarded as a variant of and of its sequences.

Presto e leggero possible*
As rapidly and lightly as possible

(1) In all other editions this eighth-note appears tied over to the following sixteenth-note; yet this is in quite evident contradiction to the "up-beat" character of both figures, which clearly are separated one from the other.

(2) This measure and the one following (in the left hand), should be practised assiduously.

* That is to say in so far as is compatible with clarity.

N. B. Essentially this is a tripart form which, however, (analogous to Invention 2), gains greater importance owing to the added canonic development. The canon, which in the beginning carries out the imitation strictly in the octave, at (a), because of harmonic considerations, leaps down to the ninth below and breaks off at (b). The (c) marks the beginning of the development (Section II), in which a livelier modulatory movement and the entrance of a relatively new figure (d), are noticeable. If, where Sections II and III meet (e), the three measures elided in order not to interrupt the movement in six — teenths were to be restored, according to the scheme of Section 1:

we would have, in Section III *an exact copy of the whole of Section I,* transposed to its lower dominant: in this way we obtain a clear general view of the fundamental plan of the form.

In addition to the light and rapid manner of playing already indicated, the performance of this "little virtuoso piece" demands the utmost precision.

Allegro non troppo, ma con spirito
Not too lively, yet with a swing

(1) With regard to the countersubject see the N. B. for Invention 5.

(2) This measure must be counted as still belonging to the *theme*, since it repeatedly appears in connection with the latter and also is worked out.

(3) The upward leap of the sixth has here been reversed in order not to remove the upper part from the medial position.

___

* The leaping eighth-notes should be vigorously struck by both hands and move in strict rhythm. With regard to the manner of performance the indication *non leggero* might well be applied. *Non leggero*, however, is quite far removed from *pesante* (heavily), just as a *non legato* by no means is synonomous with a *staccato*.

(4) Here the original: has been changed for harmonic reason; these last are especially in evidence in the second measure.

(5) A single return of the theme, extended by a closing cadence, can not be regared as an *individual section*. Hence the six closing measures at this point must either be considered part of Section II, or else must be regarded as an *adjunct*. Once evident relationship between the precedent measure (∗) and the second-last measure of the composition is recognized, one is tempted to look upon the four measures lying between as an addition interpolated merely to satisfy the feeling for symmetry.

(6) This seemingly new counterpoint is actually only a transparent variant of the first countersubject. The figure ♪♪ should sound out in a robust *non legato*.

Tempo di Giga. Vivacissimo e leggero
With great animation and a skipping touch

10

(1) With a consistently quiet wrist the finger should leave the key *before* striking the key following. This, in particular, should first be practised slowly and vigorously, somewhat in the following manner:

. These instructions, naturally, do not extend as well to the carrying out of the inverted mordents, which often are to be played *legato*, in which case only the three last notes (where they are not tied over) are to be struck *shortly*.

The carrying out of these instructions, after repeated playing of the composition, will result in a noticeable technical gain and will, in particular, further precision and lightness of touch.

(2) In order better to visualize the formal structure one should, as it were, imagine the entrance of a third, accessional part, the idea of which is approximately indicated in "reduced" form as follows:

(3) Pay attention to the analogy between this measure and the three measures following, and measures 2-5 of Section I.

(4) The leading of the upper part in this measure merely expresses the figuration of a suspension resting on the seventh, one which is resolved in the next measure: . In similar fashion, one measure later, the fundamental tone of the chord of the Dominant-Second (conceived as sustained) is embellished in the bass.

(5) This measure and the measure immediately following should be regarded merely as an "inner extension" of the movement, one which lends the melodic phrase, long drawn out, greater sweep and passion, and gives the final resolution, so to say, a certain stamp of "irrevocability". In a strictly organic sense the precedent measure is directly related to the second last measure of the composition; in which sense, it is true, the upper part must be thought of as occurring in the octave above.

N. B. The form is quite obviously a two-section one. With it all the two-part inventions which follow (with the exception of a few variants) also are in accord.

Moderato espressivo (il tocco dolce, ma pieno)
Quietly movemented and expressive (with a soft yet full touch)

11

(1) The rôle assigned the countersubject (here wellnigh raised to the importance of an independent second theme) already has been explained in the N. B. to Invention No. 5.

(2) The fugal modulation to the dominant in this place is only *apparent*, inasmuch as the theme (aside from a little deviation of the interval of the seventh, marked +) actually is answered in the tonic.

(3) The reply of the countersubject takes place in the *contrary motion*. It begins half a measure later than the original, hence on the eighth eighth-note instead of the fourth eighth-note, and proceeds from the fifth. Because of its melodic and harmonic beauty it is a most admirable contrapuntal combination.

(4, 5) To be conceived as variants of the fundamental thematic idea are: and

* Three-measure parallel passages at the end of Section 1 and Section 2, in the tonal relationship of **dominant** and tonic.

(6) In the wreathed line of this melodic figuration (to be played in a broadly expressive manner) the harmonic fundament may be recognized:

The player must strive to allow the *suspensional character* of the figuration, so to speak, "shine through".

N. B. 1. Owing to its equalized formal proprtions and its noble type of melody this invention must be accounted one of the most perfected models of its kind. It possesses a counterpart to correspond in the three-part Invention No. 7 (22).

N. B. 2. The eventual use of the embellishments in *small notes* is optional, in accordance with the player's taste.

Allegro vivace e brioso*
With great animation and sweep *

12

(1) At first, when playing slowly, the trill should be turned into a figure in thirty-second-notes:

At a very rapid tempo — and of this a really perfected performance admits — even the following would suffice:

(2) In accordance with the scale of the key of A major, in which we are moving, the mordent must choose the major second for its auxiliary note.

(3) The figure ♪♪ should be considered a variant of the theme:

* The pithy and robust "rolling off" of the figures and trills, while always observing the utmost clarity, makes per - missible a certain modern brilliancy, justified by the greater amplitude of the grand piano of our day. The **virtuoso** character of the composition, once technical infallibility is assured, even allows of a moderate employ of the **pedal.**

** See the N. B. to Invention No. 5.

(4) The *slurs* above the four succeeding appoggiature (each in the interval of a second — +), as a matter of fact, are traditional, yet not unimpugnable on this account. An uninterrupted staccato, in all probability, would be quite as valid.

(5) The Editor prefers to hasten energetically to the close, without any retarding of the tempo. Players who in this case find themselves at a loss without the time-honored Bachian "Allargando"— should they so prefer—may make use of the following ornament, to be found in the mss:

allargando

*** This case is similar to that mentioned in the note (5) to Invention No. 9.

Allegro giusto
Animated, the rhythm well marked

13

(1) In accordance with the precedent canonic scheme, it would be natural if at the two places here in question — instead of what follows — there were indicated a quarter-rest and a sixteenth-rest.

Of the four eighth-notes the *two first* notes should be somewhat more stressed, thereby allowing the imitative moment to come into its own.

(2) In many editions an A flat is incorrectly substituted for the A.

(3) The temptation to play the following: 〈music〉 as a *two-part* passage — a possibility which is quite explicable — should be resisted. The chordal figure of the "belated" quarter-note is *not* an ornamental concluding scroll; it is thematically grounded in the beginning of the third measure: 〈music〉 and thereby its real meaning is made clear.

N. B. Apparently *division into two parts* is the predominating characteristic of this form, in accordance with which each of the two parts is again divided into two *sections*.

Yet an attempt to present the piece as *tripartite* may also be justified; it might take this shape, in particular, if we establish an imaginary connection between the first half of Measure 13 and the second half of Measure 17, and, consequently, regard what lies between as a transitional passage from Section II to Section III, thus:

In this conception each section represents a separate part.

The reading given in Friedemann Bach's "Klavierbüchlein" also permits only of a *tripartite* division. In the work in question, instead of Measures 16 and 17, we have the following variants of each and then, leaping over the next four measures, we pass at once to Measure 22.

Allegretto piacevole
Not too fast, with graceful and equalized movement

(1) The thematic *figure* is composed of two interlocking *up-beat* motives, one diatonic, the other chordal, whose interconnection may be considered as assuming somewhat the following shape:

The proof of the correctness of this conception is supplied, above all, by the development in Section II (+ — +), in which *only the first* of the two motives presented is worked out. The Editor finds it advisable to treat this First Motive as the variation of a *syncopation*, whereby the rhythmic accentuation here de-manded may be secured with ease:

Inversion

It is from the triple interlocking of the figure already mentioned and from its inversion that the actual thematic *subject* results.

(2) The *answer* to the theme (thematic subject) in the dominant occurs only after a four measure (resp. two measure) interlude. At the same time it forms the conclusion of Section I, representing a sixteen-measure period. Because of its rare simplicity this form, complete in itself, by all means deserves to be called the "primal form" of its type.

(3) In the original the time-value of the **D** is doubled.

N. B. 1. The original notation takes shape as follows:

With the doubling of the note-values the presentation of the text may be said to have gained **with** regard to lucidity **and conciseness.**

N. B. 2. What has been said in the note (5) to Inversion No. 9. also, with some slight modification, applies to what follows here. In this instance we have *eight measures* instead of six; the eight, however, **in so far** as form is concerned, correspond absolutely to the six of the other inversion.

Moderato ma con spirito
Easily, yet with spontaneous movement

15

(1) The theme embraces two full measures.

(2) A *whole close* instead of the original *half-close*, in the theme.

(3) Although this incidental canonic moment is, perhaps, unpremeditated, it should, nevertheless, not be allowed to pass unnoticed by the listener.

(4) This figure and the three figures following, each comprising two quarter-notes, are a free imita-tion of the precedent thematic fragment: . To secure greater smoothness of movement, the inverted mordent has been changed to a skip of a third. In the second measure the progression of a second, on the second eighth-note (+), is inverted and becomes a descending seventh.

(5) The *answer* in the tonic is here anticipated by one half-measure.

(6) The **D** should be regarded as the seventh of the secondary chord of the seventh on the fourth degree:

Appendix
Variant of Invention I